SPEND A YEAR ON THE FARM

CHILDREN'S AGRICULTURE BOOKS

Speedy Publishing LLC
40 E. Main St. #1156
Newark, DE 19711
www.speedypublishing.com

Hello there!
Let's have a wonderful
time on the farm!

Have you ever wondered where the tasty food on your table comes from?

Kids, in this book you will learn about farming and its importance to us all.

What is a farm?

A farm is piece of cultivated land used to grow crops and raise domesticated animals.

This piece of land is important to people for it's a source of food and of other resources we need.

What is Farming?

Farming is the process of cultivating the soil. It involves planting, growing and harvesting crops.

Farming also deals with raising animals. The people who work in the farm, who grow plants or raise animals are called **farmers**.

People practice farming alll around the world. Farmers love to grow plants and raise animals.

They love the farming way of life. Farming was one of the original sources of living for people.

Farms can be so small that one or two people can tend them, or so big they require machines and many farmers.

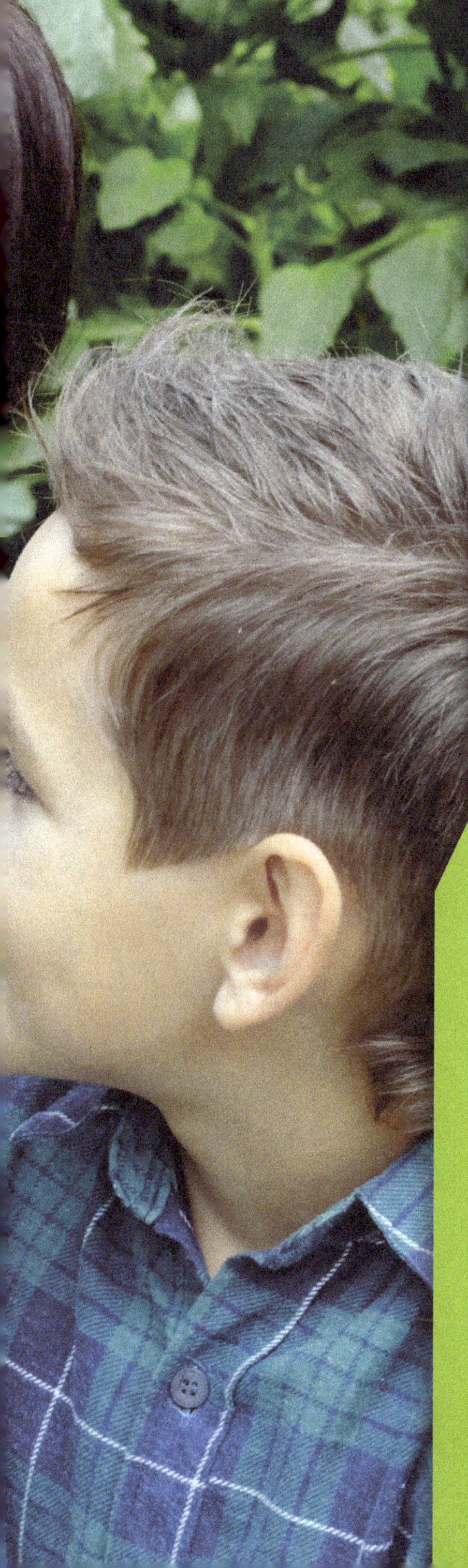

When you spend a day on the farm, you realize that farming is one of the most important things people do so we can survive and have a good life.

Once, farming was a very difficult task which required hard work and patience. Farmers had to wait and bear the tensions of uncertain weather just to know if they would have a bountiful harvest.

They did this for their family and for the whole world. Farmers have the amazing role of feeding the people.

Harvesting crops is more reliable than hunting, or gathering edible plants that grow wild. Today farming has become a lot easier than centuries ago.

Innovations in farming tools make planting, growing and harvesting more easy and more productive.

Farmers have become more resourceful over time. Innovative farming has done a great deal to improve the quality and quantity of harvests.

Farmers need to do this because they help to feed the whole world. Farmers have perfected the process of farming.

Farmers realized the important part of nature in the process. The importance of water, sunlight and fertile soil has been a motivation for people to take care of the environment as well.

Farmers do everything possible to protect the land and the harvest. Now, have you thought of spending your most precious time on the farm? Plan for it and see how marvelous farming is!

Visit
BABY PROFESSOR
EDUCATION KIDS
www.BabyProfessorBooks.com
to download Free Baby Professor eBooks and view
our catalog of new and exciting Children's Books

www.ingramcontent.com/pod-product-compliance
Lightning Source LLC
LaVergne TN
LVHW060512170826
845677LV00026B/1726

* 9 7 9 8 8 6 9 4 4 2 6 3 5 *